"Don't Kick Them Out!"

Why African American & Latino
Students Frequently Get Suspended

7 Steps to Address Negative Classroom
Behavior and Avoid School Suspensions

Dr. Jesse W. Jackson III

Acknowledgements:

To the all-star educators I have met in my travels:

Keitha Shelby and Dr. Charissa Govan
(Dallas, Texas)
Dr. Kyle Konold and Delta Academy Staff
(Las Vegas, Nevada)
Mrs. Brittain-Watts, Mrs. Hudson, and the entire
Northwest Community High School Staff
(Indianapolis, Ind.)
Mrs. Jill Ackerman, Allison Van Gorder, TJ
Winkler, and Lima City Public Schools
(Lima, Ohio)
Jon Gregory, Pamela Duckett, and the Urban
Scholars team (Columbus, Ohio)
Dr. William Logan, Mr. Adonis Blue, and the
Hillside High School staff (Durham, N.C.)
Mrs. Gloria Ford Anderson & staff
(Bronx, NY)
Richard J. Taibi and the entire Bullock Elementary
Schools staff
(Glassboro, N.J.)
Katie Hatley Tatum and staff (Little Rock, Ark.)
David Miller and staff (Marengo County, Ala.)
Dr. Karl Carpenter & staff (Alexandria, LA)

You are a great motivation in my efforts to achieve
excellence. Thank you for dedicating your lives to
educating and saving the lives of black and Latino
students in America. On behalf of the thousands of
students and parents you have helped, I want to
say thank you.

"Don't Kick Them Out!"

Why African American & Latino
Students Frequently Get Suspended

7 Steps to Address Negative Classroom
Behavior and Avoid School Suspensions

Dr. Jesse W. Jackson III

Plant A Seed Publishing & Media
Michigan * Illinois

Copyright © 2014, 2016 by Jesse W. Jackson III

Published by Plant A Seed Publishing & Media
P.O. Box 80773
Rochester, MI 48308

Printed in the USA

Visit our Websites at www.bestmancompany.com.

ISBN 978-1-938980-39-8
Library of Congress Control Number: 2015930120
3rd edition: June 2016

Discounts on books are available for bulk
purchases. To order this book, please write or
call:

Plant A Seed Publishing & Media

P.O. Box 80773

Rochester, MI 48308

1-888-987-5093
Please allow 1-2 weeks for shipping
Order online at: www.plantaseedmedia.com

Table of Contents

Introduction

Why are so many African American and Latino male students suspended from school? What is the real problem? I have exhaustively researched this issue, and I believe that I have the answer. At first glance, considering that the National Center of Education Statistics (2013) found that 82% of America's public school teachers are white, most would think it is obviously race. Ask yourself:

☐ Does your school have frequent problems with the behavior of black and Latino males?

☐ Do you find yourself or your colleagues with no options other than to suspend students for poor behavior?

☐ Does at least 70% of your teaching staff consist of Caucasian females?

☐ Does at least 70% of your teaching staff consist of whites under the age of 50?

☐ Have you been cited over the last three years for the disproportionate suspensions or expulsions of black and Latino students?

There are districts in multiple states that have been fined millions of dollars for the disproportionate suspensions of black and Latino males. If your district has any of these issues, this is the right book for you.

Similar to the corrective punishment for citizens who break the law, it is a common misconception that suspensions will teach students, who misbehave at school, a lesson to correct inappropriate behavior. Nothing could be further from the truth. The truth is that suspending students from school has severe consequences for educators. These consequences include:

☐ The loss of instructional time spent on addressing the inappropriate behavior;

☐ The shift in the amount of time allocated for collaborating with peers and meeting with parents redirected to completing the paperwork related to the suspension;

☐ The broken trust in the student/teacher relationship;

☐ And the potential racial divide between parents and some staff members that can destroy morale and promote high rates of teacher burnout.

In addition to the negative consequences that educators experience as a result of student suspensions, there are also unintended educational, psychological, and emotional consequences experienced by the suspended student. The frequent use of suspension may lower academic achievement, negatively impact self-esteem, and cause the student to harbor negative feelings about the teacher and/or school environment. Furthermore, the student may never learn the intended lesson to curtail the inappropriate behavior that resulted in the suspension. The student may simply view the suspension as a harsh punishment. Therefore, kicking students out of school, especially students who live in poverty, is the wrong way to correct misbehavior.

Don't Kick Them Out

Personal circumstances are not enough to justify not kicking a kid out for poor behavior. However, a student in negative circumstances should invoke empathy and compassion, which differs from enablement. Additionally, it is important to note that delinquent or negative behavior should not be tolerated. My experience in the prison and juvenile system assures me that our schools are our last line of defense before a prison gate or casket. If schools fail in their task to educate and save the lives of our students, then the students are doomed to poverty, a life of crime, a life in the streets, or a premature death. Consider the following statistics:

- There are over 18 million African American men in America. Over 5 million African American men are either incarcerated, on probation, or on parole.

- One of the most frequent crimes in our inner city neighborhoods is home invasion. From my experience in the juvenile system, most of the home invasions occur during school hours by suspended students or dropouts.

- The highest cause of death for African American males is homicide. More and more homicides are occurring during school hours. (Centers for Disease Control and Prevention, 2011)

- The African American male's confidence in the education process is as low as it has ever been. African American males do not believe that the education process will work out for them as evident by the 52% graduation rate nationwide. (Schott Foundation for Public Education, 2012)

A survey conducted by the U. S. Office of Juvenile Justice and Delinquency Prevention determined that of the youth surveyed in residential placement facilities, 65% had been suspended or expelled. (Chiancone, 2011).

These statistics indicate that suspending African American students from school has a negative impact on the African American community. More importantly, student suspension has an unintended economic consequence that impacts everyone.

What does this mean? Suspension may lead to a possible recession. I want all educators to ask themselves a question: what is our job as seen by our provider? The funding source for all schools, apart from private institutions, is the state and federal government. The state and federal government provide funding to educate future taxpayers.

If our students are not positioned to complete their basic academic tasks and transition into the workforce or to post-secondary education, then we as a system are failing. The government does not come out and say it in those terms, but let no one mistake how important becoming a taxpayer is. A student who is frequently suspended from school is on the path to becoming a tax taker (the American nightmare). The fact is, if these young African American and Latino boys have poor reading skills, are frequently suspended, have poor attendance, and are high school or college dropouts, they are on that path. Couple that with unemployment, and you have a recession. However, if we can keep our boys focused, improve their academic achievement, manage their behavior, increase their daily attendance, and encourage them to become high school graduates or obtain a level of post-secondary education, then we can encourage entrepreneurship and innovation, thus enhancing sustainable economic growth.

The brutal reality is that those alarming statistics, such as the fact that only 52% of African American males entering high school will graduate in four years, directly show up in the economy. (Schott Foundation for Public Education, 2012). When just three out of ten African American males complete a college degree, that hurts the economy. (American Council on Education, 2011). When over five million African American men are incarcerated, on probation, or on parole, that hurts the economy. When we have a historic level of youth murderers (particularly in Detroit and Chicago) — children under eighteen who have murdered someone — that hurts the economy.

This shows up in unemployment. The African American male unemployment rate is steadily increasing, approaching 14%. (U.S. Bureau of Labor, 2016). A lack of formal education and incarceration has a direct relationship to unemployment. Misbehavior and a student's inability to cooperate in a school setting conveys a message that the student is unable to get along with people. If a student lacks social skills and has poor academic skills, then the student will have great difficulty learning employment skills. Furthermore, if a person is incarcerated he/she is unable to contribute to the economy. This is why it is important to not kick students out of school. If the schools give up or fail, then a tax taker is launched into society.

There is a very serious economic burden that school suspensions and behaviorally based special education referrals place on society. Failure to teach educators how to approach negative conduct and find alternatives to suspensions and behaviorally based special education referrals can put a school district out of business.

When school districts believe it is okay to kick students out of school into the street rather than train them on how to behave, it will equate to financial ruin for the district. Take, for example, what has happened in the state of Michigan, particularly in many of the predominantly African American populated school districts such as Detroit Public Schools, Highland Park Schools, Inkster Schools, and Pontiac Schools, just to name a few.

One district had well over 100,000 students several decades ago, but now struggles to keep

50,000 students in its district. As a result of the decline in enrollment, many school buildings have been closed, traditional high schools have been closed, thousands of people have lost their jobs, and the school system is still trying to cut the pay of staff. Why? About 30 years ago, a negative attitude developed nationwide among educators. There was a quick trigger to suspend and remove students from school.

We have that middle-class educator attitude: "I got mine; you get yours. If you're not going to do what I say, get out of here." That mentality gave birth to the charter schools. Charter schools were started because families needed a place to send their children, whether they were the "good kids" who did not want to be around the negativity or the "bad kids" who had been kicked out of every school in town. Initially, charter schools had an opportunity to improve the educational services that were provided to students enrolled in traditional schools, by shifting paradigms. When first introduced, charter schools offered schools with a smaller student enrollment, smaller class sizes, uniforms, teachers who spent more time with students, and teachers who would work with the students at greater lengths. Now, similar to the behavior practices that are seen in traditional schools, charter schools are also kicking students out of school.

That is what has given birth to the movement. Are charter schools better than the mainstream public schools in a district? No, they are not—not most of them. Despite offering many benefits that may be unavailable in the traditional schools, charter schools are falling into the trap of using suspensions as a practice to deal with students who pose challenges. This is the same practice used by the public school systems in places like Detroit and Highland Park, in the State of Michigan, that led to the recession and ultimate school closures- kicking students out of school.

Never forget that student enrollment and daily attendance in school results in increased revenue for the district. Revenue pays salaries. I am in business, and serving my clients is how I make money. I have never understood how schools felt they could "kick out" their funding source but break their necks to get special funding grants.

Kicking "bad" students out of school has bankrupted districts around Michigan. It put Highland Park schools completely out of business. Five to seven years ago, Highland Park had 3,500 students. Now it has been taken over by the state, its high school has closed, and enrollment this past year was well under

600 students for two schools. Inkster Public Schools has now gone bankrupt, and its high school does not exist. Why? A tax base is required to fund a school system. If your school is not producing taxpayers who buy houses and pay property taxes, then you have put yourself out of business. Kicking students out and not managing behavior properly is bad for business and society.

Why Do I Single Out African American and Latino Students?

When people ask me this question, I just turn them back to the numbers. These two populations are struggling in the mainstream education system. The facts are that African American and Latinos are minorities, even though the Latino population is one of the fastest growing populations on the planet. The first major issue is that Caucasian teachers and African American and Latino students are not speaking the same language.

When we have Arab-American students, or students who come from overseas and do not speak the language, what is the first thing we do? We get a professional staff person who can speak their language. Language barriers are the reason why we are singling out African American and Latino students. There are clearly some communication barriers between Caucasian teachers and African American and Latino students. As a result of not speaking the same language, several African American and Latino students have been suspended for disruption, defiance of authority, obscenity, profanity, and vulgarity. Similarly, the breakdown in language has indirectly led to an increased number of special education referrals for African American and Latino students who have been diagnosed for emotional disturbance. I believe that due to the increased growth of the Latino population, more resources and funding is given to Latino students. Therefore, Latino male students are doing much better than African American male students. There are more professional educators who speak the same language as Latino students. There is more of a family environment in schools that have a predominantly Latino population and Latino students are getting more relevant support. They do struggle, but their needs are being addressed because the system recognizes the need to get someone who speaks their language. We do not acknowledge the difference in language and communication for African American students. While we all speak English, the difference in language can be seen in the fact that African American males communicate with a distinct style, and that is called "emotional communication." Emotional communication is not based on what you say. It is based on how you say it and whether others trust you. Children make statements like, "Do you feel me?" Forty years ago, they used the phrase "You dig?" These questions mean people are trying to be understood, trying to make a connection with the person with whom they are talking.

Many impoverished African American students are coming from homes where there is a lack of trust within the family structure. This book will clearly explain why that is and how we as educators should approach this situation.

The African American and Latino populations have specific social and emotional needs. The approach has to be very specific and direct. This issue requires a high degree of cultural and social awareness. Many people get upset about any program that might seem to exclusively help impoverished African American or Latino kids. People like to feel left out and angry that they are not being included. What I would say to anyone who feels that way is to consider the numbers. The numbers are what dictate the need for that service. This book will clearly discuss the need for this focus and provide a successful approach to addressing the relationship between white teachers and African American and Latino students.

Like all governmentally implemented policy, the desegregation of schools, the Title I movement of 1964, and No Child Left Behind all came without the necessary training for educators. When changes come to the education system, the changes should not be implemented as forced policies. We have to open the hearts of educators and help them understand why social changes and approaches have to be made. Just like students, no adult likes to be told what to do. And just like students, teachers rebel and fight changes that they do not understand.

The truth is that we need more training in this area. We do not need training on *our policies* on this matter. We need training on the African American and Latino cultures, more empathy, more personal development, and more awareness to help us better understand our attitudes toward certain people from other backgrounds and social classes.

I have been motivated by the comment of a 37-year-old Caucasian female educator who attended my training in 2013. She said that if she had known the things that I taught her in my training about educating African American and Latino males, she would have been much more effective as a teacher during her career.

She challenged me to take my message to the nation. "Every educator needs to hear this!" she said. That is why I wrote this book.

There is a high level of bitterness and anger among educators nationwide when the topic of the African American or Latino male is discussed. I respect anyone who does not have the energy or mindset to serve this population. I do not respect someone who knows this about himself but continues to go to work every day and do a disservice to this population. This book will clearly explain:

☐ Why African American and Latino students get suspended so frequently.

☐ The difference between middle-class values vs. welfare mentality values.

☐ Why the percentage of Title I students in your school matters.

☐ What is wrong with African American and Latino boys.

☐ Common behaviors for referrals.

☐ The definition of disruptive student conduct.

☐ Wrong approaches to addressing behavioral problems.

☐ Why special education is not the answer.

☐ Why students disrespect teachers.

- ☐ The 3 things a student wants to know.
- ☐ The 7 teacher personality types.
- ☐ When are suspensions necessary.
- ☐ The 7 Ws of how to manage negative student behavior.
- ☐ How to decrease African American parent and Caucasian teacher conflict.
- ☐ The 21 dos and don'ts for solving disruptive classroom behavior.
- ☐ The 12 laws of classroom etiquette.
- ☐ The 7 stages of negative behavior correction.

If you have questions, this book has specific answers. If African American and Latino male behavior issues have been a problem for you in the past, this book will give you the knowledge to strengthen your approach to correcting negative student conduct. Let's get to work.

Chapter 1
What Is Wrong With African American and Latino Boys?

Understanding Their Problems

Why do African American and Latino boys have a higher rate of school suspensions, academic failure, dropping out, violent deaths, juvenile delinquency, and incarceration? The reason is that African American and Latino families have the highest rate of children living in a home without a father. Orthner (2006) writes that "more than 68% of black children are born to unmarried parents, with half or more of these children not having significant contact with their fathers after they reach three years of age."

Nearly 2 in 3 (66%) African American children live in father-absent homes. Nearly 1 in 3 (33%) Latino children live in father-absent homes.

-National Fatherhood Initiative-

Research shows that living in a fatherless family damages a boy's self-esteem. The truth is, being raised in a home with your father translates to being a stronger person. What this means for African American and Latino boys ranges from them having problems in school to participating in gangs as part of their search for male role models (Neenan, 2000).

The father-child relationship is the most vital relationship in every human being's life. It will determine both a boy's emotional stability and his personal development. Why did God give us all fathers? Every father has 10 primary God-given roles and responsibilities. They are:

1. To protect.

2. To discipline.

3. To provide financial means.

4. To build and maintain his children's self esteem. To fill his children with courage, boldness, strength of purpose, and confidence.

5. To provide guidance and education (financially, emotionally, socially, and about relationships).

6. To teach children the proper respect for their mother.

7. To protect the virginity and sexual purity of all his children.

8. To be directly involved in the marriage transaction of his children. (To prepare his son to be a husband and his daughter to be a wife, and to give her away).

9. To be a role model and example in conduct and choices.

10. To provide unconditional love.

All of these responsibilities are what a father means to his children, and these are the things many African American and Latino boys are lacking. When most of these needs are met, humans generally have emotionally healthy and fulfilled relationships. Today, we can see that this is not happening. More than ever, boys are looking to the streets and to girls to fill these voids.

If your father did not do these things for you, it does not mean you cannot succeed in your career or life goals; however, it does mean that you will have a spiritual and emotional void.

When any one of these 10 essential needs is not met, or is met on a minimal level, the individual (regardless of gender, race, or economic background) will suffer from "daddy issues," or in clinical terms, the "Without-a-Father Syndrome." The Without-a-Father Syndrome is defined as the negative emotional, mental, and physical response to growing up apart from, separated from, with a lack of closeness, or without the desired connection or relationship with your biological father. The Without-a-Father Syndrome is a lack of *emotional* love from our fathers. Emotional love develops self-esteem and confidence. Emotional love and many emotional issues are deceptive and dangerous because they are not readily visible; they can be hidden or masked for extended periods.

Everyone needs love, and we all have a primary method through which we best receive that love. This is our love tank, and this is where the love is stored. Just as cars take different types of gas, people take different types of love. Dr. Gary Chapman, the author of *The 5 Love Languages*, teaches us that there are five primary methods of love distribution. They are:

• Words of affirmation (words of love).

• Quality time (time spent with a person).

• Receiving of gifts.

• Acts of service.

• Physical touch (hugging, kissing, and affectionate rubbing).

Essentially, our love tank operates by this process:

Love

- Words of affirmation
- Quality time
- Receiving of gifts
- Acts of service
- Physical touch

The Pump

(Love in action)

The Tank

(Our heart, soul, and mind)

The Average Love Tank Is Empty.

An empty love tank causes us to be *"Love Deprived,"* the most dangerous state a human being can live in. The lack of emotional love characterizes the Without-a-Father Syndrome as the reason for most societal ills or dysfunctions, including:

☐ Poverty

☐ Behavioral problems

☐ Crime and delinquency

☐ Premarital sex

☐ Emotional distress

☐ Teen pregnancy

☐ Violent crime

☐ Child abuse

☐ Incarceration

☐ Substance abuse

☐ Gang violence

☐ Dropout rate

☐ Drug and alcohol abuse

Consider the following statistics noted on the Fatherless Generation website:

☐ 85% of all youth sitting in prisons grew up in a fatherless home (Fulton Co. Georgia jail populations, Texas Dept. of Corrections 1992).

☐ 80% of rapists motivated with displaced anger come from fatherless homes (*Criminal Justice and Behavior, 1998*).

☐ 70% of juveniles in state-operated institutions come from fatherless homes (U. S. Department of Justice, 1988).

The numbers don't lie. Many people with these problems do not realize why they have made these choices. All of these behaviors and actions are emotionally driven, and without our fathers meeting our emotional needs with love, acceptance, and confidence, we are forced to meet those needs on our own.

It is important to point out that every circumstance and response to that circumstance is different for each individual. However, certain behaviors are predictable. For example, most boys who were abandoned or rejected by their father will likely display some level of entitlement, anger, and hostility in their behavior. The same holds true for most girls who were rejected or abandoned by their father; they tend to seek unhealthy affection from boys at an earlier age, which often leads to premarital sexual relationships. It is important to understand that the Without-a-Father Syndrome has different forms:

- [ ] Type I: I don't know my father, or he is deceased.
- [ ] Type II: I know my father, but he does not acknowledge me.
- [ ] Type III: I know my father, I lived with him, but he was unable to provide what I needed.
- [ ] Type IV: I had a substitute father.
- [ ] Type V: I was born out of wedlock.

Society assumes that problems occur only for those who grow up without a father in the home; however, the Without-a-Father Syndrome suggests that an individual who grew up in a home with a father will display the same or more destructive attributes as a fatherless person if the 10 essential father roles and responsibilities are not met. This is the root of our students' behavioral problems.

There is nothing we can do to change the family circumstances of our students. However, fully understanding the emotional issues of our students can allow us to be more empathetic and not take their negative conduct in such a personal manner.

Chapter 2

Why African American and Latino Students Get Suspended So Frequently

Frequent suspensions are a product of an ongoing social class conflict. I call it the "middle-class mentality" (Caucasian teachers) vs. "welfare mentality" (impoverished African American and Latino students). Let's thoroughly break this down.

First, ask yourself, what percentage of your student enrollment includes students who are eligible for Title I funding? If it is 30% or higher, then the "middle-class mentality" (Caucasian teachers) vs. "welfare mentality" (impoverished African American and Latino students) is your reality. The common challenges of impoverished Title I students frequently include:

☐ The devaluation of education

☐ Manipulation

☐ Taking advantage of the situation

☐ Challenging authority

☐ Poor work ethic

☐ A lack of order

☐ Disrespect for the process

- Substance abuse
- A lack of confidence
- A lack of employment skills
- Poor reading skills
- Anger and hostility
- Hatred of authority
- Not getting along with peers
- Not following instructions
- Engaging in criminal activity
- Not taking education seriously
- Engaging in sexual misconduct
- Depression
- Major family issues
- Learning disabilities
- Low self-image

When students deal with poverty, these are the challenges they face. If you're in a district with 80% or more Title I students, you also are likely to have a high African American and Latino population (not all the time). Ask yourself, are we fighting poverty, or are we fighting race? We're fighting poverty. Poverty has been masked and painted black and brown, but it really is incumbent on us to take a conscious and detailed look at the damage done by how we view our students. I've got news for you. No one likes poverty. I don't like poverty. I don't like being around it. When our kids are impoverished, they bring an impoverished mind, an impoverished spirit, and an impoverished learning attitude. This is where conflict stems from.

What most educators don't know, or fail to comprehend, is that poverty has more of an influence on us as professionals than we understand.

Working with economically disadvantaged students and parents has had a negative effect on educators. Many educators have been disheartened by the frequent misuse and abuse of benefits that many parents receive. It is insulting when a hard-working person who struggles to make ends meet sees people who don't work every day receive money, free food, and housing assistance by manipulating the system. The spirits of many educators have been broken, and morale is low, because professionals are not seeing the results they want. We got into the helping profession because we wanted to see people's lives change, and we're not seeing that happen. Actually, it appears that our students are getting worse. This is the type of thing you've got to watch out for as a teacher. A lot of times, you're giving your heart and soul and you're not seeing the results you want, and that can be very depressing or make you bitter.

I want you to think about this.

☐ We've got over 25 million children today who are living separated from their biological fathers.

☐ Grandparents have become the dominant primary caregivers for the Title I population.

☐ Over 65% of Title I students come from a single-parent environment.

☐ About 40% of our students come from a home with an incarcerated parent or an incarcerated relative.

☐ Sixteen million American children are struggling to receive daily meals. That is the Title I student population. The majority of the behavioral problems that we encounter can be attributed to a lack of proper nourishment. Hungry students act up.

When you check your behavior reports and your suspensions, check from the first of the month to the tenth. You will see that the rate of reports will be relatively stable or much calmer for that time period, after families have received their welfare benefits, but when you tally the reports from the 11th to the 30th days of the month, you will see changes in behavior—more arguing, more aggression, more fights. When do most of the problems occur in a school? It's always early morning and after lunch. When they get that snack, their body does not respond like yours does because, unlike you, they are not accustomed to eating three delicious meals a day. Once they get that nutrition—and it may not be the best nutrition—it doesn't greet their body well. It actually agitates them because the body is trying to hold on to the food it has. We have to pay more attention to the hunger issues of our students. They are affecting behavior. Thousands of the teachers I have trained confirm that they see this happening.

☐ When you see these behavioral problems, it's because most of these kids come from fatherless (or disconnected) homes. That accounts for 85% of the behavioral problems. [Center for Disease Control]

☐ Approximately half of all mental health disorders occur before age 14. These are our students, so we have to look at the matter from a mental health perspective, particularly focusing on depression.

My professors taught me to always think about depression first whenever we suspect a mental illness. Now, think about the things we just discussed. Do you think these things wouldn't depress you? Absolutely, they would, and that is only the onset. Most depressed people are going to do one of two things: totally shut down or act out. That's what you're seeing, and we don't know how to manage it.

Middle Class Values vs. Welfare Mentality Values

Throughout my professional career, I have observed that there are many teachers-particularly Caucasian, middle-class teachers-who are very angry about how impoverished African American and Latino students are treated. Why is that? My research has shown that well over 80% of teachers come from *poor* or middle-class working backgrounds. Hearing about how *poor* people should be treated is an immediate trigger to them because they themselves were raised *poor*. They look at themselves and say, "Well, I was *poor*, and I didn't have a lot, but I got an education and did something with my life. Why are we giving things to people who take advantage of it and don't appreciate it?" I present to you that many of us who are now educators grew up poor, but we did not grow up in poverty. What is the difference? If you were raised in a family that didn't have a lot of resources, but your parents had a vision for you, or you had a vision for yourself, of the way education could change your life, then being *poor* just meant not having money. Poverty, however, has a distinct difference: poverty is a mentality, and it is deeply rooted in your values and your spirit.

What is the difference between rural poverty and the poor African American poverty that we see in the inner cities? The answer, very simply, is *welfare*.

Welfare is a mental crutch. Welfare has mentally crippled people with the mentality of having "just enough to get by." It has also created the entitlement mentality. As a matter of fact, most human services benefits are called entitlements. Entitlement means you are owed something. This is an atrocious message to send because the system does not owe them anything. It's a dangerous mentality. It is one thing to help the poor, but it's another thing to enable people to manipulate and take advantage of the system. We, as professionals, have to understand what we're dealing with and overcome it.

The government has spent $13 trillion over the past 30 years to aid the poor, and this has created an incentive for people to remain poor because they know they will get help. A person who is content with being poor becomes impoverished. A poverty mind is a scarcity mind. A scarcity mind will take what it can get. If the families are not working for it, they feel like they are winning and all of us who go to work every day are fools. That's what the poverty or welfare mind has created. It has enabled people not to work and to receive something for doing nothing. It's made people become deceitful and find ways to manipulate the system.

Welfare Facts That Have Devastated Poor African Americans

In 1964, President Lyndon Johnson launched the "War on Poverty," enacting a level of antipoverty legislation never before seen in the U.S. and adding many new dimensions to the American welfare state. In his June 1965 speech, the president suggested that the problems of African Americans' problems could not be solved through self-help alone, stating, "You do not take a person who, for years, has been hobbled by chains and liberate him, bring him up to the starting line in a race and then say, 'you are free to compete with all the others.'" This was his view of African American people. Discover the Networks states:

☐ A Cato Institute study noted that welfare programs for the poor incentivize the very behaviors that are most likely to perpetuate poverty.

☐ As a FamilyScholars.org report puts it: "When a couple's income nears the limits prescribed by Medicaid, a few extra dollars in income cause thousands of dollars in benefits to be lost. What all of this means is that the two most important routes out of poverty — marriage and work — are heavily taxed under the current U.S. system."

☐ Martin Luther King, Jr. said, "Nothing is so much needed as a secure family life for people to pull themselves out of poverty."

☐ A similar study by Mary Corcoran and Roger Gordon of the University of Michigan concluded that the more welfare income a family received while a boy was growing up, the lower the boy's earnings as an adult.

☐ The out-of-wedlock birth rate among African Americans today is 73%, three times higher than it was prior to the War on Poverty.

- In 2010, blacks (approximately 13% of the U.S. population) accounted for 48.7% of all arrests for homicide, 31.8% of arrests for forcible rape, 33.5% of arrests for aggravated assault, and 55% of arrests for robbery.

- Also as of 2010, the black poverty rate was 27.4%, meaning that 11.5 million blacks in the U.S. were living in poverty.

The historical facts show that the relationship between President Lyndon Johnson and Dr. Martin Luther King, Jr. completely broke down over this issue. Dr. King was adamantly, vehemently against welfare because he knew what kind of effect it would have on human development.

Dr. King believed that welfare would destroy black people and hinder their progress. Fifty years after that legislation was launched, we can see that Dr. King was absolutely right. The facts show that welfare has created an *impoverished* mindset in poor African American people. The reality is that more African Americans are living in poverty today than before the war on poverty began.

This is important for understanding people who get upset and say, "Well, I was poor too." It is critical to understand that our students lack much more than just money. How can we see that? We can see it in terms of values.

Here are some characteristics of the values of the middle-class and welfare mentality populations that I believe will provide clarity to some of the problems that we see with students at school. I call it "middle-class values" vs. "welfare mentality values."

Middle-Class Values	Welfare Mentality Values
1. Education	1. Devaluing education
2. Marriage	2. Cohabitation
3. Marrying before having children	3. Having children for income or security
4. Accepting authority	4. Challenging authority
5. Going to work every day	5. Having a poor work ethic and attendance
6. Order	6. Lack of order
7. Respect for the process	7. Disrespect for the process

8. Happy-hour drinking	8. Substance abuse
9. Employment skills	9. Lack of employment skills
10. Keeping it together (holding emotions inside, taking medication to cope)	10. Anger and hostility (outward anger at authority figures)
11. Ability to get along with peers	11. Inability to get along with peers
12. Ability to follow instructions	12. Inability to follow instructions
13. Forty-hour work week	13. Hustler mentality
14. Family issues managed at home, if possible	14. Family issues likely to lead to family separation

These are the differences in values that have created a breach between the middle-class or working-class teacher and the student with a welfare mindset. We see a lot of students who have a higher value for their social worker than their teacher. Why?

The child welfare system gives you a social worker. You have a case worker for every family. It is possible to have more connection and contact with that person, and that person tells you, "If your teacher does or says something to you, you let me know." The child therefore thinks this person has more authority than the teacher. In many cases, this has caused a breakdown in the partnership between the teacher and social worker. What this has also done is given birth to "income-driven" special education programs, which families use to increase their income. It's a welfare mind that thinks, "Let me get you on some medication. Let me get my kid tested and get him into the special education system."

This practice extends the welfare benefits for the family. It happens frequently whether a family is African American, Latino, or Caucasian. It gives a person a manipulative mind, and that person learns to take advantage of and manipulate the program. One of the characteristics of people who are *impoverished* is that they've learned how to manipulate others and how to take advantage of their situations. They've learned how to get around the rules. Once people learn the rules of welfare, there are some people who will want to take advantage of the rules, they'll want to manipulate the system.

Please understand that welfare has helped a lot of families. Thousands of poor families have taken advantage of the welfare benefits until they could get on their feet and change their situation. What I am highlighting is the enabling mindset that individuals use to their advantage. This is the population we are confronting today.

The Onset of Disproportionality

"The Middle-Class Female Social Worker" vs. "The Impoverished African American Mother"

I believe President Lyndon Johnson's 1964 antipoverty legislation gave birth to disproportionality as we know it today. This legislation gave the social worker authority over the mother who was receiving welfare. In 1964, a middle-class social worker who worked for the government was likely to be a Caucasian female. To get welfare in 1964 and 1965, you had to be an unwed, poor mother. There are a lot of dynamics you have to understand here, because society was not very kind to this mother, and her own community was not very kind to her. We have to understand that this middle-class, female social worker was not very kind to her either.

Think about it during this era, African American families on welfare were likely assigned a middle-class social worker (likely a Caucasian female), who was likely to be married and have children, judging and assessing another woman who was poor, who had kids out of wedlock, and who couldn't feed or take care of her kids. That relationship was very judgmental, and it was very damaging to the woman's self-esteem. One of my senior advisors is an eighty-four-year-old white female who was one of those social workers. She describes being trained to go into homes and check the closets to see whether there were men's clothes in them, in order to find out whether a man lived there.

One of the ways they liked to threaten the mother was to say, "If you don't clean this house up," or "If that man is living here," then "I'm going to take your benefits." Well, what happened? People started learning how to lie and manipulate the system. We had fathers who were sneaking into the home where their children lived to see their kids and their partner. We had social workers disrespecting those men because they didn't have resources and couldn't take care of their kids.

Those types of policies attached to receiving aid made men who already felt bad about not being able to take care of their families feel worse. This contributed to decreasing fathers' involvement in the lives of their children and promoted an unhealthy relationship between impoverished men and women.

The relationship with that Caucasian, female, middle-class social worker was a judgmental one, and fifty years forward, we can still see that judgmental attitude. This is why so many Caucasian female teachers and African American and Latino, impoverished or working-class mothers don't get along. The residue of those ideas still exists. It's still prevalent, and it's a part of the way the two parties view each other.

There are many impoverished African American mothers who teach their kids — and I quote — "Don't listen to that white woman. If that white woman does anything to you, tell me." In their minds, they believe that the teacher is judging them. This mindset is the result of the feelings and beliefs that linger from the introduction of the 1964 legislation. One of the key elements of the No Child Left Behind (2001) legislation was to increase shared accountability between schools and parents. As a result of this legislation, parents were provided information related to children's education, teacher qualification, and the quality of the schools that children attended. However, despite using the information to make shared, well-informed, educational decisions, the residue of the unresolved social class war between the middle class professional female and the impoverished mother has continued and even escalated. We see impoverished parents coming to the school, cussing principals out, cussing teachers out, wanting to fight security, and wanting to fight teachers. I can remember being thoroughly embarrassed as an African American man when I saw dozens of impoverished African American parents lining up to insult school board members and the superintendent of a local school district where I worked. They had to have security guards and the police at school board meetings. It was as if it was okay to take out your life frustrations on the school system in public. This is a manifestation of their pent-up anger at themselves. However, they see the middle-class females as the problem and vent their frustration on them. Typically, the male administration and staff is not treated with this level of disrespect. This gives an indication that many of these problems have a gender undertone.

What a lot of our middle-class female teachers do is look at the mother and notice that she goes to great lengths to make sure that her kids are well dressed, that she's well taken care of, that her hair is done, her nails are done, and she has a nice car. She's finding a way to take care of herself. It makes many middle-class female teachers envious, and they say, "Well, I go to work every day, and I have two college degrees, but my kids don't have True Religion jeans. My kids don't have Michael Jordan gym shoes. I don't drive a new car. How did she get that?"

When the teacher gets jealous of the mothers, it creates further conflict. I presented this idea to one thousand educators who were Caucasian females, and 100% of them said, "Yes, you're absolutely right. When I see that, it does bother me." Why is that? **The middle class is trained to compare.** In the middle class, you're taught to look at what other people have and to assess yourself by what other people have: "If they have two new cars, we need two new cars. They got a new house; let's get a new house."

That's what the middle class does because that's the way they were trained.

White Guilt

The other side of the welfare mentality is the white guilt paradigm. By definition, **white guilt** is the guilt felt by some Caucasian people for harm resulting from racist treatment of people of color by Caucasians, both historically and currently.

I have met many Caucasian teachers who suffer from this white guilt. First of all, any guilt that we hold for the actions or attitude of others is inappropriate. Guilt is an emotion that occurs when a person feels or *believes*—accurately or not—that she has violated a moral standard. Guilt is a negative emotion. White guilt is a mentality. I truly understand white guilt because there is something called "black guilt." This is where African American people try to make other African Americans feel bad about being successful in a certain area of life. Some believe that as an African American, you owe other African American people something because of your success. This is where we hear the term "give back." African Americans who do not comply with this expectation are called "sell-outs." This is a mental vice for many African American people, making them feel duty-bound to give or do things that are not necessarily in their heart to do, in order to make others happy.

The same is true with white guilt. We have to ask, where is the guilt coming from? Are you guilty because you or someone in your family shared negative racial views? Is this guilt controlling you and your decision-making? Do you work with African American and Latino kids out of white guilt? Were your parents racist? If so, do you feel guilty about that?

A very good friend, who is a Caucasian female administrator in Texas, confided in me that while growing up, her father had frequently told her and her siblings that "black people were stupid." She said this gave her the inspiration to become a teacher and help African American students. As great as that sounds, it is a serious problem. That is the foundation of white guilt—emotional motive! I always tell my college students that they should choose careers based on their life purpose, not a trauma (negative event) that they have experienced. Even if we believe that our motive is just or justified, it impacts our attitude. If you set out to help "poor black kids" and they don't accept your help, two things will happen: your feelings will get hurt, and you will become resentful. I believe this is unconsciously happening to thousands of good teachers, both African American and Caucasian. There are thousands of African American teachers who went into education to make a difference because of their personal background. They feel that they come from the same background as the student and can therefore make a difference.

There are also hundreds of young Caucasian middle- and working-class teachers signing up to work with organizations that offer education services to poor inner-city students, most of whom are African American and Latino. We have many public school districts and charter school organizations that have schools in urban neighborhoods with 99% poor African American and Latino students, while their teaching staff is 99% white. They employ African American people in the roles of dean of students, behavioral support, security, and social workers, but not in the classroom, where the battle is fought. **Ladies and gentleman that is true disproportionality.** I truly believe that most of the decisions that create this disproportionality are completely unconscious. My job is to make us aware of this issue. It is my hope that awareness can cause people to change their approach.

Anywhere you find black or white guilt or resentment, you will find a high level of disproportionality in school suspensions and special education referrals for African American and Latino students.

Chapter 3

Common Behaviors for Referrals

Some of the common reasons for giving behavioral referrals are profanity, willful defiance, and fighting. The first paradigm shift that I need us to understand is that fighting is not a good reason for a behavioral referral. Once individuals get involved in fighting with other students, they have reached another level of rule violation. They are engaging in criminal conduct. That has to be thoroughly explained to students at the beginning of every school year and explained again through monthly reminders. This is not twenty or thirty years ago, where two kids could fight and the administrator would bring them back for a conference to shake hands and apologize. We live in a society where parents and family members get involved in the fights of kindergarteners. There have been several cases where the parents of kindergarteners have come to blows over an altercation between two five-year-olds. We must look at the issue of fighting differently. Having a lazy approach and saying, "Well, that's just kids being kids," can result in someone getting killed.

Disruptive Student Conduct

We must define the term "disruptive student." If you asked one thousand educators to define "disruptive student," I can safely guarantee that you would get at least seven hundred different answers.

A disruptive student by definition is an unproductive student. Disruptive students do not do work and fail to complete academic assignments. When a student is unproductive, he becomes a disruptive student and his behavior becomes a problem. School is about learning and doing the tasks and assignments that have been set forth by the teacher. If the student is not doing those tasks, that makes him disruptive because his behavior is inconsistent with the reason that he came to school. That is the basis of how we make all of our behavior-related decisions. A student who is not doing his work is engaging in the initial behavior that we are tasked to stop. We need to stop it with five-year-olds, and we need to stop it with fifteen-year-olds.

Teachers get caught up in the emotional stimuli of what students do and say. They don't look at the bottom line, which is always production. School is about teaching and learning, and all students are tasked to do their work.

Method Of Discipline

Therefore, if a student suffers from behavioral problems, why would we punish him? It means that the kid doesn't know how to behave. Fifty years ago, there was a term called "home training." In the 21st century, many of these kids are not getting home training, so they're coming to school untrained. If this is a deficiency that the teacher sees, it becomes his or her job to make a mental adjustment.

When a child has behavioral problems, it denotes an unmet emotional need, which is a lack of home training. Home training is in part love and nurturing. Why should we punish children who are just showing that they don't know how to act? *What would we do if the kid didn't know how to read?* **We would teach him to read.** Well, folks, these kids don't know how to act, so we have to teach them how to act. Sending students home will never show them how to act.

If a youth fights, why do we suspend him? Once again, the behavior is caused by not knowing how to get along with people. Once the youth crosses the line and feels that he can touch people, he's entering into a new system (juvenile detention). I believe that we can correct a lot of the fighting and physical misbehaviors early by changing our approach to punishing them.

If a student uses profanity, why would we suspend him? He has proven that he has a limited vocabulary. Wouldn't school be the best place to go to improve his vocabulary? I would hope so. We allow students to put their heads down, and we say, "Be quiet if you're not going to learn."

I present to you the idea that a student with his head down in a classroom is just as disruptive as a student who keeps getting up and interrupting the teacher. School is about learning and performance. It is not a place to sleep; it is not a place to do anything but learn. We as educators are duty-bound to correct and stop these errors.

Punishment does not correct disruptive conduct. This is why our prison system is a complete failure. While there are people who do need to be in prison, we need to understand that no one goes to prison in order to correct their own behavior. That is why the prison system gives conduct violation tickets to inmates. Prison is a punishment. Suspensions are punishments that produce the same results: reoccurring behavior or withdrawal.

Additionally, we have educators who believe that they can buy the cooperation of their students with rewards. They believe that students should be rewarded for doing what they asked him to do.

Rewards send the message to the students that they need to be incentivized before they can do anything. I think that we have to be very cautious about the messages that we send when we offer rewards. Rewarding students for good behavior often produces entitlement.

Chapter 4

Wrong Approaches

Here are some forms of discipline and approaches to suspensions that I know are completely wrong and can only make behavioral problems worse.

Ten-day suspensions. This practice is criminal. They do not correct misbehaviors. They exist for the professional's benefit, not the benefit of the students. Some educators believe that the parent will fix the child's behavior problem and the parent will be inconvenienced if a student is assigned a suspension that lasts for multiple days. Nothing is further from the truth. Suspensions that last multiple days have resulted in daytime youth home invasions in the inner city.

In-school suspensions that remove students from the classroom to work in another part of the building. In-school suspensions are completely ineffective without appropriate *behavior training*. We will discuss the effective way to execute in-school suspension programs later in this book.

The color system. The color system is used in the adult and juvenile penal systems.. This is a model that we use to train prisoners. I'm asking all professionals to reevaluate this approach and decide if they believe it is a good idea. Educators are entitled to do what they believe works, but, at some point, all of our practices must be reassessed. Students must be trained to respond to the verbal and written instructions of the teacher. I have seen students, even young students, manipulate the color system by doing just enough to obtain a color to get a reward. I believe that the color system does not promote personal growth. It is like the difference between short-term vs. long-term. Behavior issues are not problems that we want to mask or temporarily stabilize. Our desire should be to grow and develop our students for a productive existence in society, not just our environment.

Special education. I once met a school administrator whose school policy was to refer any African American or Latino boy for special education if they had a behavior problem. This is exactly the kind of mentality that we are fighting. This is a complete misuse of a very important educational service. Any belief that special education should be used for behavior problems is completely erroneous. The next chapter is dedicated to exploring why this practice is inappropriate.

Chapter 5

Special Education Is

Not the Answer

"I'm not stupid, Dr. Jackson!" This is what one of my incarcerated fifteen-year-old high school students said to me passionately. "I have been to seven schools, and nobody can help me because they don't listen to me." When I asked him why he thought people didn't listen, he responded, "Because I'm always upset. I know I don't read well, and when I've worked with teachers in the past, they've made me feel stupid. I'm not stupid, Dr. Jackson," the young man said.

After that conversation, I had this young man reevaluated, and the results showed that he was not in need of special education. He had walked around with a stigma and a negative approach because his mother had always told him, **"Don't ever trust white people."** The young man arrived with an angry disposition toward white people, who were the predominant members of the special education staff in the district, and he never cooperated with them.

This is important because our cultural norms and our ability to communicate in our relationships dictate how we evaluate students. The process begins when a child is identified as possibly needing special education and related services. The person who makes the referral is typically the student's classroom teacher. Differences in personality and style of communication can create serious problems.

If the person who makes referrals for special education does not relate to the student, they will make a referral based only on their values or feelings about the student's conduct, instead of the student's need for special education services. **A Caucasian woman from a middle-class background evaluating impoverished African American or Latino boys who are angry, use profanity, and were taught not to trust Caucasian people can easily become a problem**.

When we deal with issues of emotional disturbance and learning disabilities, all the judgments we can make are extremely subjective to the evaluator. According to the Office of Special Education & Rehabilitation Services state 31% of (students) who have been admitted into the special education program have been diagnosed with mental retardation. Mental retardation is something most professionals can physically see. It can be seen in the face and the motor skills, and it can be heard in the speech. In this book, we're not discussing the mentally disabled. We are instead discussing the emotional disturbances and learning disabilities that account for roughly 60% of special education referrals.

For admission to special education, students are evaluated, typically by a psychologist or psychiatrist. Nine times out of ten, that person is an affluent, high-earning American citizen who is not black or Latino. Less than 2% of the psychiatrists and psychologists in America are black or Latino, so typically that is not who is there. (Surgeon General's Report 2001.

African American and Latino students are not typically evaluated by someone from their culture or social class who identifies with the norms of that culture or social class. Once a child is found to be eligible for services, the individualized education program (IEP) meeting is scheduled and the IEP is written. Typically the IEP meeting includes the mother, the impoverished child, and the middle- and upper-middle-class education professionals.

The professionals at that table have education and come from middle-class backgrounds. If these professionals work in a Title I school, the parent sitting across from them is poor. In many cases, that parent makes less than $10,000 a year of accounted income. Frequently, the assistance parents receive is tied to their children's special education needs. There is no discouragement for accepting the special education service. Instead, they're given an outright encouragement, in that it turns into income.

What happens with most of our students is that the first IEP they have stands forever. It becomes a lifetime sanction. **I have always said that boys need more help than girls.** Boys are high-risk. More boys are represented in special education. In fact, according to Dionanna Ricks (2016), boys make up more than 67% of all special education students. Boys account for 71% of all school suspensions, and African American and Latino boys account for 59% of those school suspensions. The special education population is 80% black and Latino boys. These are some brutal realities. The fact is that either there's a problem with our boys, or there's a problem with us. Obviously it is us. We need to carefully evaluate this process. Again, I don't believe that much of this is done consciously. However, if a consistent practice is proven to cause long-term harm to students, then we should re-evaluate it immediately.

Most Common Referral for African American and Latino Male Students

The two most common special education referrals for African American and Latino male students are attention deficit disorder and emotional disturbance (anti-social personality disorder).

Attention deficit disorder is the most common special education referral for African American and Latino boys, and I believe it is totally misrepresented and commonly misdiagnosed. By its definition, attention deficit disorder falls into different categories — inattention, hyperactivity, and impulsivity.

A person who has attention deficit disorder may have some of the following symptoms: difficulty paying attention to details; tendency to make careless mistakes in school and other activities; tendency to produce work that is messy and careless; high level of distractibility by irrelevant stimuli; inability to keep attention on tasks and activities; difficulty finishing schoolwork, paperwork, and other tasks requiring concentration; frequent shifts from one uncompleted activity to another; procrastination; disorganized work habits; forgetfulness in daily activities (for example, missing appointments or forgetting to bring a lunch); and failure to complete tasks such as homework and chores.

Hyperactivity symptoms include fidgeting, squirming when seated, getting up frequently to walk or run around, running or climbing excessively when it's inappropriate, appearing restless (in the case of teens), having difficulty playing quietly or engaging in quiet leisure activities, and often talking excessively.

During my training sessions, I ask, "How many people here have sons?" Half the participants raise their hands. Next, I ask, "How many of you have experienced these characteristics in your sons?" Everyone who had a son raised his or her hand. These are common characteristics of boys. These are the characteristics that most boys exhibit, particularly when boys are not supported, guided, encouraged, and parented consistently. We must make sure that boys are coached and encouraged away from certain conduct and habits.

How can we lower this level of attention deficit conduct? It's called parenting. It's a matter of who is supervising the child and helping him cope with those natural, common traits of a young boy. **Not of a black or Latino boy, that goes for any boy.** Boys are hyperactive, boys can display inattention, and boys can be impulsive. **The difference in boys**

from different backgrounds is what parents do in coaching and training their sons.

Folks, this is the great problem of special education. Our boys are not being parented. We need to spend more time evaluating their parents. It's difficult for untrained 5-, 7-, 9-, 11-, or 13-year-olds to raise themselves, particularly when it comes to education. Education requires a large amount of discipline from parents. When parents don't know how to discipline their child, to slow him down, or to call for attention and focus, that child will lack discipline. A lot of students who are referred for special education are untrained children. They are emotionally neglected children. They don't have a learning deficit; they have a social training deficit, and that is what's causing the problem.

Another common special education diagnosis is antisocial personality disorder (emotional disturbance). Every young man who I have worked with in juvenile detention was diagnosed with antisocial personality disorder, and his conduct supported the diagnosis. Here are the traits of antisocial personality disorder: a persistent pattern of thoughts, feelings, and behavior that are described differently from what is considered normal in a person's own culture. That statement right there tells you what the problem is. If you haven't been parented and you haven't been trained to behave properly in school, then the value you place on education and your education etiquette will be lacking. Thus, if you have a child who has not been taught to sit still, follow instructions, and obey authority, that child will exhibit the characteristics of antisocial personality disorder. It is the parent's job to teach those behaviors and to impose them on children. If the children aren't learning from their parents, they will have symptoms of attention deficit disorder or antisocial personality disorder, simply because they're being raised in a disorganized and dysfunctional culture. They bring that culture to school and let it interact with a middle-, working-, or upper-class American teacher. They intertwine their own culture with that of someone who has different values. That difference in value systems creates conflict, which leads to increased student suspensions, lack of productivity in class, and fallings-out between our teachers and students. This has a direct correlation to a large proportion of our referrals for emotional disturbance.

Antisocial personality disorder is specifically a pervasive pattern of disregarding and violating the rights of others. It may include symptoms such as law-breaking, lying, starting fights, not feeling guilty or taking personal responsibility, and acting irritably or impulsively.

Since there is no specific, definitive test that can accurately assess the presence of antisocial personality disorder, healthcare professionals conduct mental-health interviews in which they look for antisocial symptoms. If the cultural context of the symptoms is not considered, antisocial disorder (emotional disturbance) is often falsely diagnosed.

Research indicates that minorities tend to be falsely diagnosed with antisocial personality disorder, resulting in less treatment and more punishment for those individuals, often in the form of school suspensions. If left untreated, people with antisocial personality disorders are at risk of developing or worsening in multiple other mental disorders. Those with antisocial personality disorder are also at high risk of dying from homicide. This is a brutal reality, and it means that this issue is a serious problem.

Emotional disorders have become more frequent and now make up the majority of the referrals that I encounter. For true mental illness and emotional disturbance, the need for such referral is irrefutable. We've seen the emergence of the emotionally impaired population, and it really has no precedent outside of the spike in children being diagnosed with attention deficit and antisocial personality disorders. Their environment has left them under-trained, neglected, and under-nurtured. The standard American educator is untrained to identify these characteristics. Thus, they approach this problem with a lack of awareness, which increases our referrals.

In addition, many of our special education departments contradict themselves by following their schools' standard suspension practices. Even after a kid gets put into special education, he can still end up suspended and expelled. This reality tells us that the current special education practice does not address issues of conduct.

We have had a decade of inappropriate, ineffective, or marginally successful practices that have led to the suspension and referral to special education for thousands of African American and Latino boys. These practices, have firmly placed African American and Latino males on the prison pipeline because some educators took the path of least resistance. For ethical reasons, I'm asking all of us to stop these practices. These practices might make it easier for you in the short-term, but society will pay the price later.

Chapter 6

Why Do Students Disrespect Teachers?

One critical question that we need to ask ourselves is, "Why do students disrespect teachers?" The answer is simple. When we see students who are disrespectful to teachers or principals, use profanity, have disruptive conduct, or fail to follow instructions, it is clear that they do not respect that individual or that environment. There is no way around this fact. Now, this is not as offensive as one might first think. Some kids don't respect themselves, and some are taught not to respect teachers based on race or gender. This is a brutal reality. At the same time, this situation challenges educators to be people whom the students respect by carrying ourselves like emotionally mature adults. Unfortunately, there are teachers who struggle in this area. There are teachers who struggle with low self-esteem, and they therefore attempt to befriend their students or interact with them passively. Children know when this is happening, and many like to take advantage of this behavior just as they would if it were shown by a parent. If you're not a self-confident educator who can command respect, students will run you over, whether you work in the urban schools, the rural schools, or the suburbs.

Chapter 7

Three Things a Student Wants to Know

There are three basic questions that are very important in a student's decision of whether to respect a teacher or not. One of these is the question, **"Does this teacher care about me?"** I know a lot of teachers who do care, but they don't have any idea of how to show this feeling. Their interpersonal skills are so flat that they don't know how to communicate caring to a child, and that child can see it.

Secondly, a child may ask, **"Can you, as the teacher, help me?"** The final question is, **"Are you the kind of person who I can trust?"** These three critical questions are the primary reasons why our educators are so disconnected from their students. The children have asked these questions, and the answer to all three, in regards to many teachers, has been, "Absolutely not."

It is our job as educators, to be people whom students can trust, whom they feel can help them. The fact that you went to college and got a teaching job does not mean that people trust you or believe you're competent. The reason why some teachers do really well in the field is that they know how to manage people. The teachers who are struggling do not know how to manage people. Most don't even manage themselves very well. They're emotionally sensitive and easily offended. Their bosses offend them and the parents offend them; even five-year-olds can offend them by refusing to accept their approaches. These are educators who go to a training lecture and look for a reason not to listen to the presenter. When colleagues try to help them, they become defensive and sarcastic. That, folks, is a sign of personal and professional immaturity. I call it an "un-teachable spirit." This type of person not only fails in managing negative classroom behavior, but also fails in personal relationships with colleagues, partners, and his or her own children.

Chapter 8

Teacher Personality Types

I've been able to identify seven types of teachers according to what I call their basic personality types. There are certain personality types that will conflict with the Title I population or be easily taken advantage of by the students. What I want you to do here is to be very honest with yourself and see where you fit in. Here are the seven teacher personality types:

1. **The Passive-Aggressive Teacher.** No one will want to say that they're passive-aggressive, but if you're a teacher who avoids conflict on all levels, this is you. This is a teacher who wants to keep the peace. This teacher is like a parent who won't engage to stop unacceptable conduct in the home. She wants to be the teacher the student likes. That's a losing philosophy.

2. **The Enabling Teacher.** This is the middle-class teacher who works in urban America, especially with poor, African American, and Latino kids, and wants to rescue them. This teacher feels so bad about the student's story and what they've been through that he fails to impose discipline in order to protect the students from more hardship.

This teacher enables students by having low expectations instead of pushing students to learn and become great. The teacher with low to no expectations is the great student enabler.

3. **The Taskmaster Teacher.** This teacher is rigid. She expects what she says to be done. No exceptions. She doesn't play around. Students come into her classroom, and it's all business. This teacher makes the students work every second that they are in class, every day. This is the taskmaster teacher.

I don't try to change this kind of teacher. I've had teachers like this. They can hurt people's feelings, but one thing we have to say about them is that they get results.

4. **The Mean-Spirited Teacher.** These teachers are miserable in their own lives, and being tough on kids makes them feel good. They think it's cool to be rude to them. Most students have encountered a mean teacher. Students know them when they see them. These teachers need to remember that these are just children. Even a 17-year old is just a child. Students often ask, "What's her deal?" "What's his deal?" "Why is he so mad?" Who wants to be around a mean teacher? If you're this kind of teacher, check yourself.

5. **The Rookie Teacher.** You know this one. This is the teacher fresh out of college who believes that the stuff he was taught will work for a Title 1 school in an urban district. He's just totally delusional. The rookie acts like a rookie: coming in, bouncing off the walls, showing no humility, being unwilling to listen, just a bundle of sensitivity. If we try to point something out to him, he gets sensitive and emotional. He feels like, "You're just putting me down." He cannot accept feedback. The rookie teacher has an over-reliance on his education. However, education will not teach you how to emotionally deal with difficult students. Employing people smarts, the ability to relate well with others, will yield greater results compared to relying on book smarts, especially when interacting with disadvantaged students.

6. **The Idealistic Teacher.** This is the person who really understands the full scope of teaching. This is the teacher who wants to serve humanity. Students have problems, but this person is committed to helping students solve their problems. This teacher wants to understand and help students. This is a wonderful person to be around. This teacher always has a good, upbeat,

positive attitude about helping others. This is the kind of teacher that most students love to have.

7. **The "I Want to Be Your Friend" Teacher.** This is the worst teacher personality! It bears repeating: This is the worst! This teacher thinks that she is friends with the students. Listen, if this is you, you're going to have to make a serious adjustment. Typically, the teachers who want to be their students' friend do the same things with their own children: they're trying to be friends with their children. I do not want those people anywhere around me, because they will always compromise our mission. We are not here to make friends with the students. That is a lack of discipline as a professional. We also see this type of personality in educators who have sex with their underage students. This is a crime. Needing to seek the approval of a child is an emotional disorder, which should be monitored very closely by administration.

The first step in improving yourself as a teacher is to recognize your personality type. Identify the kind of person you are and what kind of personality you bring to the classroom. I can tell you right now, a passive-aggressive teacher will not succeed in communicating and working closely with an impoverished African

American or Latino student, particularly in a Title I school or an impoverished school. An enabling teacher makes the situation worse.

Mean-spirited teachers will always cause relationship conflicts. Mean-spirited people tend to have a quick trigger and want to put students out.

The idealistic teacher has more success working with the impoverished African American and Latino populations. The rookie teacher is 50/50. Some get it and catch on quick; some don't. The "I want to be your friend" teacher is an abject failure. This personality type has no chance of being successful in education or parenting.

Identifying these teacher personality types is central to planning how we move forward.

We want to work together with our students, not keep up a wall. Be honest: Acknowledge your personality type. If your personality is one of the types that make the situation with our students worse, then identify it, acknowledge it, and make some adjustments.

Chapter 9

7 Ws of How to Manage Negative Student Behavior

When analyzing behavior, you first have to figure out the seven Ws, *the first being what the behavior violation is.* I need to know what the student did wrong so I know what we need to correct. Too many times, however, educators cannot convey what the behavior violation is. They say the child is angry or he has a bad attitude, but that's not a behavior violation. We need to determine, what is the negative behavior that needs to be corrected?

Once we find out what the violation is, we need to find out the second W: *Why is the student acting out?* What is the root cause of the behavior dysfunction?

The next step is to determine the third W: *When does the negative behavior show itself?* Is it more commonly seen in the morning? After lunch? If we know when it happens, we can chart it. If we know when we find it happening, we can nip it in the bud.

Similar to knowing when the behavior happens, we need to find out the fourth W: *Where is the environment when the child starts acting up?* Is it specific to one classroom? This is important to watch out for because, for many students, their behavior is classroom-specific.

Students may act one way in one teacher's classroom, then another way in another teacher's classroom.

This leads us to the fifth W: *What is it about you that makes the student act up in your classroom?* If a student exhibits a problem in one teacher's classroom but not in another teacher's class, you need to determine why. I was at a school once with ten teachers, only two of whom didn't have problems. Why? They had better relationships with the students and better management of their classrooms. If you move that person out and put a new person in, (i.e., a sub), you'll see all kinds of behaviors popping up. What is it about you that allows that? What is it about you that makes a student conduct himself in this unhealthy, unproductive manner? This is un-reviewed data. We know the student has a problem, but what is it about us that perpetuates the problem?

Next, we need to ask ourselves the sixth W: *What are the consequences if we let this behavior go?* What will the consequences be to our life and to the student's life? I can give you a clear idea. If you've got a high number of suspensions and expulsions, you are feeding the future of high incarceration. You are feeding your competition—the juvenile facility—which is taking students from public education and consuming time-and-a-half funding (meaning tuition plus some). This is the reality, and the consequence is that you have to say you produced a tax-taker.

We know the parent is the one who is supposed to coach kids and bring them to us ready to teach, but that is not happening. So what do we do? Complain? Then the parents blame us. There is no room for complaining in this competitive world of education. You need a solution. We need to evaluate and make adjustments. If we cannot manage it, we are just contributing to the problem.

Finally, we need to find out the seventh W: *Who or what is triggering the behavior?* Knowing what triggers the behavior — the fighting, the blurting out, and the negative, disrespectful conduct toward a teacher — allows you to understand the scope of the error so you can correct it.

Knowing the triggers also gives us a more comprehensive method of dealing with discipline onsite. This is a new skill that teachers have to develop. We believe this gives you a framework for understanding and identifying ways to maintain an ongoing position from which you can identify and solve behavioral problems.

Chapter 10

21 Dos and Don'ts for Solving Disruptive Classroom Behavior

When Are Suspensions Necessary?

Suspensions are absolutely necessary in certain situations. Therefore, we should have a consistent philosophy about when to employ them.

I'm asking that we reevaluate the rules and the systems that are already in place, because the systems that are in place may benefit adults and not students. I'm charging us to reevaluate how we do things. Here are fourteen questions that I believe will help us to better understand our views of and approach to student conduct. Please answer these questions honestly.

1. Has a student ever made you cry?

2. Have you ever wanted to physically grab a student?

3. Have you ever had an argument with a student?

4. Have you ever challenged a student to a fight or to follow through on a threat?

5. Have you ever suspended a student?

6. Has a student ever made you want to physically assault him?

7. Has a student ever made you want to quit your job?

8. Have you ever threatened a student?

9. Have you ever physically touched a student?

10. Do you believe that some students need to have their butts kicked?

11. Have you ever used profanity in the presence of a student?

12. Do you believe that students should not talk back?

13. Have you ever felt threatened by a student?

14. Has a student ever made sexual advances toward you or made you feel sexually uncomfortable?

Your answers to these questions will give insight into your core beliefs about student behavior and school discipline.

I have developed 21 dos and don'ts that I believe all teachers must live by to improve classroom management and to discourage and defeat negative behavior. These are the things that I know will help you.

1. **Reestablish yourself as an adult.** Due to the failures of many of our students' parents, many of our students don't know how to respect or interact with adults. Many students, even at young ages, are raised to act as adults. Parents don't know how to parent, so they raise their children as if they were their siblings. They talk to their children as adults. These children are involved in their parents' business. They're allowed to use words that children shouldn't use. They're allowed to do things that children shouldn't do. Why? Parents might have limited time to spend with the child, and as a result of this limited time, parents choose to not focus on discipline. Also, children experience more unsupervised time at home. This all leads children to act as if they're adults. It's important for teachers who work with these students to establish themselves as the adults. You have to talk to these students and literally tell them, "We're not peers. You call me Mr. or Mrs." You have to establish that with them, because we have a culture of students who have devalued teachers, and who see them as babysitters.

2. **Explain the role of a teacher.** Clearly define the role of a teacher to the student and their value to society and to the world. Establish yourself as an authority (an expert). You have to let the students know what you do as a teacher. Unfortunately, many students don't know what the teacher's role really is. A lot of them think, "I have to go to school because my parents make me," and that's how they live. You have to say, "I am the teacher, and this is what teachers do for students."

3. **Document your expectations of students.** All teachers should set high expectations for their students and publish them for all students to see. While working with fifty-one violent juvenile offenders over seventeen years of age, I made it mandatory that everyone earned a GED or high school diploma, and that they all read one book a week. Prior to my tenure in the facility, only two students had graduated from high school in ten years. During my three-year tenure, we graduated twenty-seven young men with high school diplomas or GEDs. If given a chance, students will meet your expectations. African American and Latino males can learn, behave, and graduate. Set expectations and make them known.

4. **Accept responsibility for your classroom.** I expect that every person who enters my house must, in turn, respect my house. When problems arise in my house, I don't call the landlord, I fix the issue. Similar to owning a house and taking responsibility of the things that happen in your house, teachers must accept responsibility for the classroom. When you own the classroom, you don't have to call the assistant principal or dean of students.

5. **Be consistent.** Consistency will always win. Avoid giving students breaks. Giving students breaks will open the door for you to be taken advantage of. Don't give breaks.

6. **Avoid sarcasm.** Sarcasm is repressed anger that you're trying to let out softly. You'll never win the respect of a student with sarcastic, slick answers. You're actually angry because the student offended you, and you're trying to get back at him with sharp words. It's inappropriate, and that is not a very adult or professional way to manage yourself when interacting with a student.

7. **Establish personal boundaries.** I've noticed many teachers who don't have personal boundaries. This is why we see so many teachers having sex with students. Students are in the teachers' personal space- on their desks, playing with their phones, hugging them, and doing all sorts of things that are inappropriate. Personal boundaries are vital to being able to elicit respect. One teacher, whom I recently met, has tape around her desk. She makes sure that her students know this is her area and her space, and the students know not to cross that line. It's just the way it is. Boundaries are vital for keeping the behavioral structure in place.

8. **Do not argue with students or parents.** When you argue with a student, it shows that you are out of control and that you have lost control of the situation. Arguing shifts the control to the student and indirectly communicates the message that you're being controlled, even dominated. You really have to go about things in a totally different way, because arguing just doesn't work. Any time you argue with a student or parent, you—the teacher or administrator—always lose.

9. **Do not antagonize students.** Don't be the kind of person who antagonizes students to try to correct negative behavior. The student is wrong. Why would you try to antagonize him, causing him to make worse decisions and to commit worse violations than he already has? It's our job as educators to be a part of the solution, not to come down to the level of the misbehaving student. Antagonizing suggests that we have come down to the level of the child. It's immature, unprofessional, and inappropriate. We have to stop it, particularly if we don't want the students to act that way. Don't be an antagonist.

10. **Don't yell at students.** I've been amazed by how many teachers believe that its okay to yell at students. Raising your voice shows that you're out of control. When you're yelling, you're telling the student that he has triggered you. When the student sees that you're out of control, he does one of two things: he becomes frightened, or he feels joy. Either way, you lose. Yelling at students and losing control of your tone will always cause significant problems for you and will cause students to lose respect for you. You have to watch your tone.

11. **Don't use profanity.** Unfortunately, many professionals believe the use of profanity around students is socially and professionally acceptable. Nothing could be further from the truth. The use of profanity by an education professional really is peculiar and shows a lack of tact. If you don't know how to use professional language to get your point across as an educator, then it's wise to get help.

12. **Don't put your problems off on someone else.** This means you should not call the administration or the dean of students, as if you expect the administration to help or even to make a student show respect. Some teachers believe in using this as a threat. They say things like, "I'm going to call the principal on you." You can't expect anyone to make a student respect you if you say that. As teachers and educators, we have to be able to handle our own problems. Educators who rely on calling the principal are considered a burden to the staff.

13. **Be verbally appropriate.** I've seen emotionally offended teachers make extremely inappropriate comments. I've seen teachers allow themselves to get so

frustrated with students that they use poisonous words. They make slick comments; they say things that are just completely inappropriate. You shouldn't tell a student that he is "never going to be anything" because he doesn't respect you or his work. You shouldn't tell a student that he or his parent "is poor or broke" and that they're "never going to be anything." You shouldn't tell students that they're "stupid" or "dumb." I've found these types of comments to be completely ineffective. It is very important for our teachers to control their emotions and their tongues in every situation.

14. **Do not have a verbal and emotional meltdown.** This happens to folks who get so emotionally wounded that a student can cause them to emotionally break down in the class. They start yelling, they start screaming, and they say, "Get your things. Get out of here. Get out of my class right now. You're not staying in here one more minute." They completely embarrass themselves in front of the other students and their colleagues. This is an entirely inappropriate way to conduct yourself with students.

15. **Don't challenge students.** If a student is being aggressive, challenging the student to a fight or other negative conduct is the wrong approach. One of my district superintendent colleagues in North Carolina once told me that he had to suspend a teacher because the teacher had challenged a student to a fight. The teacher told the student that he was going to "kick his ass" because the student was trying to "act like a man" and challenged him to a fight, to which the educator said, "Do it." These are the kinds of things that we can avoid. These are the types of situations that are spurred on by pride. Pride will make you a bad teacher. Pride will ruin your career. One of the things that you want to make sure you do is live a pride-free life as a teacher. Sometimes our students will do and say things that are inappropriate. Remember, our students are in the process of growing and developing. Because they're still growing, we always have to be adults and make sure that we keep control of the situation.

16. **Do not lie to or about a student.** I think too many of our teachers lie about students. They do this after the student offends them or hurts their feelings. A lot of teachers feel

like they have no other recourse than to conjure up a story to get the student removed. I have seen teachers lie about students. I have literally seen them plan to set students up. The teacher who does this does not reflect a high level of character and integrity. This is the worst kind of teacher and, quite frankly, they should not be teaching. Do not let this be you.

17. **Do not take out your frustration on a student.** Folks often get very upset, lose their cool, and take out their anger on kids. If you're frustrated and a student is getting to you, do not be the kind of professional who takes out that frustration on a child. Many of our suspensions are direct responses to the professional frustration of an educator. We see teachers who actually hold grudges against students and suspend them on that basis. This is the sort of thing that we absolutely have to avoid. It is dangerous behavior. There are no winners when teachers do this, which brings us to the next point.

18. **Don't hold grudges.** Unfortunately, teachers are some of the most unforgiving people in the world. They hold grudges.

They remember what a student did when he was five years old. One of the things you want to make sure of is that you're not the kind of person who holds grudges against children, remembering everything they did wrong. That is a guaranteed way to ruin relationships and your classroom culture.

19. **Forgive and forget every day.** No matter what goes on between a teacher and a student in a day, we need to forget it and start every day with a clean slate. However, most teachers don't do this. I had one colleague say to me, "These teachers have to know, when does the punishment stop?" We have seen teachers continually punish students. They want to ensure that they remember the lessons they've learned. If you want to gain respect and decrease negative conduct, I do not suggest that you conduct yourselves in this way.

20. **Do not give your energy to disruptive students.** I have seen school buildings taken hostage by a single disruptive student, who was able to control the climate and culture of the entire building. When this happens, it is a complete error on the part of the administration. It is within our

grasp, within our reach, to control the behavior the student is exhibiting. I've seen school staff give a lot of energy to students who do the wrong thing, who just want everyone's attention. Don't give your energy to a disruptive student. Disruptive students have to be reflective and taught how to become aware of what's going on with them that makes them act that way. That's the only way you can work with this type of student. Students have to be made aware of their negative conduct so they can change it. They don't need you to give it energy or to put special programs in place to deal with it.

I worked at a school that paired a new teacher with a young, first grade, six-year-old African American boy who didn't comply with the directives of the new teacher. The school's intervention was to tell her, "Whenever he acts up, press a button in your room and send him down to the resource room so he can sit in there and do his work with the resource staff." This means that this one student was controlling all of the adults. He dictated how the day went for them. This young boy learned how to manipulate adults. The truth is, this practice was just making it harder on his next teacher or his next school. This, folks, is the wrong way to manage behavior. **There is no way around teaching students how to behave.** (The next section of this book is dedicated to that concept.)

21. **Implement the Twelve Laws of Classroom Etiquette (the Behavior Model).** The most common question I'm asked is, "Dr. Jackson, what do we do? If you tell us not to suspend him and not to remove him, what should we be doing with him?" Simple. **Do what we do for a living:** *Teach him!* When we wait until a student has done something wrong, we're being reactive, not proactive. The first step that we like to take in my school during the school year, when the students come back in August after the summer break, is to engage in what I call "classroom behavior orientation."

Classroom behavior orientation is simply teaching students appropriate classroom etiquette. I developed the Twelve Laws of Classroom Etiquette for classroom behavior orientation. The Twelve Laws of Classroom Etiquette are:

1. Go to class every day.

2. Arrive in class on time.

3. Enter the classroom silently.

4. Have your supplies.

5. Listen to your teacher.

6. Follow the rules the teacher makes.

7. Raise your hand to get permission to speak.

8. Don't use cell phones or send text messages in class.

9. Don't sleep in class.

10. Don't touch others.

11. Don't touch others' property.

12. Don't disrupt others.

I have found that several students have no idea how to conduct themselves in a four-wall classroom. This training has to be given to them in a small assembly. You can't teach it by passive-aggressively placing signs on the walls, sending letters home, or passing the burden from one teacher to the next. No, you have to present it as a model of classroom etiquette for the whole building, and you literally must teach students how to conduct themselves in an academic setting.

I had to do this very thing at several colleges because the conduct of the students was so egregious. Why was their conduct so poor? At many of the previous schools where they attended, the classrooms were out of control. The students did not learn appropriate classroom etiquette. Once again, if home training is absent, we have to supply it ourselves. In the past, the home was the first place where children learned how to behave. Today, that's not the case. It is the job of each teacher to set the tone for his or her classroom, and the administration must set the tone for the whole building.

I suggest conducting behavior assemblies on the Twelve Laws of Classroom Etiquette at least four times a year and, in the process, communicate, to the entire building, what is and is not acceptable. Some schools should literally do this every single month.

Behavior orientation and the teaching of classroom etiquette is the best way to lay a foundation for consistently productive behavior. I have been asked how we go about doing this with five-year-olds. We do it in exactly the same way. Twenty years ago, if you wanted students to learn a special topic, you would take them to an assembly and share it with them: "Don't talk to strangers," or "Say no to drugs." School assemblies, group learning, visuals, and interactive presentations are still the way that this has to be done. This learning does not occur on a classroom-to-classroom basis. The message has to be clear, consistent, and practiced by everyone in the school.

The first step is to teach the Twelve Laws to all the professional staff. I have found that too many teachers don't live by the Twelve Laws of Classroom Etiquette. Expectations vary from classroom to classroom. Getting the staff to live by these laws is the most important thing if you expect results.

Ultimately, practicing the 21 Dos and Don'ts is essential when addressing disruptive student behavior. You'll notice that all of these changes are personal. We have to make personal adjustments to negative conduct if we ever want to see successful outcomes.

Professional and personal development is required to carry out this monumental task. I hope that these twenty-one practices set you on the path to success.

Chapter 11

How to Decrease Parent and Teacher Conflict

During the age of the No Child Left Behind movement, the relationship between low-income, Title I African American parents and Caucasian, female, middle-class teachers has dissolved. I have developed some basic conflict resolution principles for both teachers and parents. I hope that these ideas can help us to work better as a team and end the conflict.

1. **Acknowledge personal problems.** Teachers can help decrease conflicts with parents by acknowledging that many parents have personal problems. Don't take it personally.

2. **Respectfully address parents' issues.** Many Title I parents already feel inferior, so teachers should never portray an attitude that makes the parents feel belittled. Many times, Title I parents expect the worst and, even if a teacher does not suggest an inequality, they twist words so it appears the teacher is being disrespectful. Teachers need to practice how to respectfully take a step back because, a lot of times, parents will try to bombard us and engage us in a

negative way. We've got to stay a step ahead and always be respectful when addressing parents. Teachers should be assertive and respectfully address the issues while always staying professional.

3. **Support parents' needs.** Increase the time and resources spent on supporting parents' needs, such as using Title I funds to help all parents get a GED or high school diploma.

4. **Keep parents informed.** I know a lot of good schools that have parent email lists, and this ensures that parents are always in the loop. Email is informative. Sending notes home with kids is prehistoric and doesn't work anymore. Look for more effective ways of communicating, whether it's uploading notes on Facebook or using the school's website. Keeping parents informed via text messages or email is very powerful and gives the parent no excuses. Maintaining this communication can also prove helpful in achieving what teachers are trying to do.

5. **Understand the uniqueness of education.** Education is, first and foremost, a business, but its business side has been neglected for many years. People do not want to see education as a business, but it is. The thing

that is unique about education is that your client is also your boss. Without students and parents, a teacher doesn't have a job. They're not like customers who come to you to buy something and are happy to be there. A lot of times they are there by default. You have to manage that fact to be more productive and make the outcome more favorable for you.

7. **Principals have to be highly skilled in creating an environment of harmony and teamwork.** Principals should never take sides, but should always seek resolution and work to keep parents and teachers happy. This balance is critical in the education process. We specialize in helping principals and parent organizations to create a better working environment in order to improve student learning and academic achievement. If your school needs help in this area, call us at 888-987-5093 or visit us at www.bestmancompany.com.

Parents and teachers should work together as partners. Both parties rely on each other to do a job. Parents need teachers to educate their children, giving them a chance to be successful in life. In turn, teachers need parents to support their efforts and respect their work. **If** parents and teachers fail to work together as partners, the education system will not succeed. Today, the parent-teacher relationship is the worst it has ever been. To change this situation, parents and teachers must once again come back to the table as partners. Take this action step: Allow parents to attend school staff meetings. This builds trust in the parent/teacher relationship.

Teachers should be able to resolve all problems they might have with parents. It's not easy, but it is doable. These steps will lead to a decrease in conflicts between parents and teachers.

Chapter 12

7 Stages of Negative Behavior Correction

When examining the stages of correcting negative behavior, it is important to ensure that three components are in place. First, you have to correct the students' behavior. Second, you have to correct the teachers' behavior. Third, you have to correct the parents' behavior. There are seven questions that each of these parties has to answer. The following questions should be addressed in every in-school suspension or behavior correction class. Here are the stages and the steps you should take students through.

Stage One: What did I do? The student has to accept responsibility for his behavior. The student has to verbally say, with his mouth and in writing, what he did. If the student has not done this, we don't have any basis for improving his behavior. In a lot of these situations we're doing all of the talking. We complete the student's paperwork, and we do all the administrative work that comes after; the student isn't doing any work. Even at five years old, the student should have to answer a series of questions that probe into the inappropriate behavior, and he must acknowledge verbally and in writing that his behavior was wrong.

Stage Two: Why is the behavior wrong? The student has to explain and put in writing why the behavior is wrong. What this question does is require the young person to process his own negative conduct in order to understand why he did what he did. When students answer a question and reflect on why their behavior is wrong, they're learning. Answering questions and being interviewed will prompt a student to think. We want our young people to think. This is how we correct negative behavior. Once the young person can see why the behavior was wrong, we've turned a corner.

Stage Three: Why did I do it? Young people need to understand why they did what they did and they should make an emotional connection with the feelings that were unleashed through the behavior. Be specific when asking students why something happened. Questions such as, "Why did you have that tantrum?", "Why did you bite that person?", "Why did you punch that person?", "Why didn't you listen to me?", and "What were your feelings when you were ignoring me and my instruction?" should be asked. These questions take students through the emotional awareness of how they feel when they act a certain way. That's what we have to do in every single occurrence of inappropriate behavior in order to bring about the correct behavior. This is a pivotal part of the behavior-correction paradigm.

Stage Four: Who taught me that? Every student, whether five-years-old or eighteen-years-old, should be able to reflect on who taught him the learned behavior. Knowing how the student picked up the negative behavior is vital. Knowing the source of the inappropriate behavior allows you to eliminate the behavior at its roots.

Stage Five: What will happen to me if I continue with this negative behavior? What will the consequences be? Have the student write down all of the things that will happen to him if he continues with the negative behavior. We call this "creating new ways," as it allows the young person to counter his own negative behavior by recognizing its impacts.

Stage Six: Why shouldn't I do it? Sometimes young people don't believe that what they've done is wrong. Ask the child, "Do you feel that you shouldn't do it? Tell me why or why not." Until students can identify what they did wrong and know that it was wrong, they will never reach the point of correction. This is pivotal to correcting behavior.

Stage Seven: What kind of person am I, what kind of life do I want for myself, and does this behavior fit that life? Ask the student to write the answers to these questions and say the responses to you. Again, what we always want students to do is evaluate their own conduct. Stage Seven is the aftercare and reintegration part of the process. This is where the student can return to the normal classroom. This means that he has gone through all seven steps of the program and is now prepared to successfully reintegrate into the classroom.

Suspending a student just delays the inevitable. These are the things that I know can help us avoid suspensions and better serve our young people. Nonviolent offenses can be corrected with this intervention.

Students who commit violent crimes have to be locked up (or detained for a period of time), regardless of their age. You cannot allow students to hit or put their hands on anyone else. Once a person learns how to assault people and get away with it, they're addicted. This kind of conduct has to be stopped. If we let young people learn that they can get away with certain things, we're basically developing a felon who believes it's all right to hurt people.

I encourage all of you to take a hardline stance on violent behaviors, like fighting and bullying. When you see someone who has this sort of problem, particularly in elementary schools—someone who likes to fight, who's very angry, and who says, "So-and-so made me mad. That's why I punched them"—you are duty-bound to stop that conduct. The student won't get better over time. The only way they can get better is with the proper training. Behavior problems are happening, but students aren't getting the training that they need to improve; they are getting suspended.

We must place emphasis on behavior training, not suspensions. The dean of students, all administrators, and all teachers need to be trained to teach our students how to properly behave. We have too much tolerance for physical violations and not enough patience to learn how to properly address the behaviors that we can change, like profanity and willful defiance.

Our ability to properly identify, respond to, and manage the inappropriate behaviors that are displayed in school might help to reduce in-school and out-of-school suspensions. The practices that have been presented in this book are tools that I know work. I thank you for reading. I look forward to working with you soon.

About The Author

Dr. Jesse W. Jackson III is a nationally recognized school behavior consultant and therapist who specialize in at-risk student achievement and criminal behavior prevention. Dr. Jackson has been in private practice since 1998. As a keynote speaker, seminar leader, and licensed professional counselor, Dr. Jackson addresses more than 100,000 people each year.

Dr. Jackson has authored 52 books, 11 of which have become international bestsellers, including the male developmental classics *The Best Man, College or Prison: The Male Crisis of The 21st Century, Black Males Can Graduate, Black Males Can Learn, White Teachers, Black Students, Can We Keep Black Boys Out of Prison?, "Don't Kick Them Out!", Divorce Is Not An Option, Educators & Money, How to Prevent Educator Burnout, I'm Tired of Being Broke,* and *Success or Failure: Leaders are the Difference.*

Dr. Jackson has been instrumental in founding the Daddy Issues (Without a Father Syndrome) and Momma Issues (Oppressive Mother Syndrome) diagnosis and treatment model. Dr. Jackson has embarked on a journey to help the members of this fatherless generation heal the emotional wounds from their failed or unfulfilled relationships with their fathers and mothers. Dr. Jackson teaches individuals how to identify the symptoms of these syndromes and walks his students through the spiritual and emotional detoxification healing process. Dr. Jackson's exhaustive research on the effects of paternal disconnection and absence on children's confidence, emotional stability, and ability to learn has been respected and cited by his colleagues and students throughout the nation.

Dr. Jackson has been in private practice since 1998. Dr. Jackson has continued to excel in helping school districts, organizations and colleges find effective solutions to improve at-risk students academic achievement and graduation rates. To contact Jesse or his staff directly, use the following information.

Mailing Address:
The Best Man Company, LLC, PO Box 80733, Rochester Hills, MI 48308
Toll Free: 888-987-5093
General Inquiries: info@thebestmancompany.com
For Inquiries Related to Events, Interviews, or Speaking:
Angela Smith, Director of Operations:

info@bestmancompany.com

Seminar and Workshop Requests:
All sessions include an evaluation and three books for all professional staff. All parent sessions include one book for each parent participant.

Bulk Order Requests:
To order Jesse W. Jackson III's books, including *Black Boys Can Learn*, *College or Prison*, *Don't Kick Them Out*, and Pay Attention, visit
www.plantaseedmedia.com, or your local bookseller. For orders of 50 copies or more, email us at info@plantaseedmedia.com. Bulk discounts on orders of less than 50 copies are not available.

2016-2017 "School Culture" Professional Development Program With One Of America's Foremost Experts In At-Risk Student Learning & Performance, Dr. Jesse W. Jackson III

Do you want your staff to stay motivated, inspired, and productive all year long?

Does your school have behavioral challenges with at-risk students?

Does your staff need support and instruction on how to work with difficult students?

Does your staff face challenges with classroom management?

Does your school want to effectively serve students of all races and ethnic backgrounds?

If so, then this is the best professional development program for your staff.

Dr. Jesse W. Jackson III has established a reputation for excellence in the area of professional development for the twenty-first century educator or human services professional. Dr. Jesse W. Jackson III's professional development program focuses on strengthening the core values of our schools with teamwork, professional ethics, professional values, diversity, and high-quality instructional practice by promoting healthy lifestyles for staff members. As society has presented our colleagues with more challenges, Dr. Jackson has come to specialize in providing the best solutions.

This program consists of 16 sessions:

1. **"Don't Kick Them Out!"** How to Manage and Address Negative Behavior Problems

2. **How to Improve Results (Outcomes) with the 21st-Century Adjudicated Youth**

3. **Anger and Aggressive Girls!** How to Help Female Students Stay Focused on Academic Achievement

4. **7 Steps To Improving Standardized Test Scores**

5. **Why Boys Hate School:** How to Teach and Engage Difficult Male Students in the Learning Process

6. **How to Decrease Parent–Staff Conflict**

7. **How to Improve the Attendance of 21st-Century Title I Students and Parents**

8. **White Teachers, Black Students:** How to Effectively Serve Students from Different Racial and Ethnic Backgrounds

9. **"Who Is in Control?" The Pillars of 21st-Century Classroom Management:** How to Create a Powerful Learning Environment

10. **How to Improve Teamwork and Build a Team Culture in a Professional Staff**

11. **Am I a Better Teacher This Year?** How to Refocus the 21st-Century Educator on the Mission of Education

12. **How to Manage and Address Challenging Behaviors and Personality Conflicts**

13. **How to Build a School That Meets the Needs of the 21st-Century Student and Parent**

14. **Pay Attention!** How to Improve Classroom Instruction with 21st-Century At-Risk Students

15. **College or Prison:** How to Educate, Discipline, and Keep African American Males in the Classroom and out of Prison

16. **How to Have the Best School Year of Your Career:** Staying Motivated, Healthy, and Productive All Year

Level 5: Last Chance School
Professional Development Training Packages

Service Type	Gold	Platinum	White House
Number of Professional Development Sessions	4 sessions of choice	8 sessions of choice	12 sessions
Books and Materials	100 books of choice(from Dr. Jackson's 25-book library)	200 books of choice (from Dr. Jackson's 25-book library)	400 books of choice (from Dr. Jackson's 25-book library)
Number of Parent Sessions	1 parent session	2 parent sessions	3 parent sessions
Student Success Assembly	1 student success assembly	2 student success assemblies	3 student success assemblies
Location	At your school	At your school	At your school
Session Interchangeability	You can interchange sessions	You can interchange sessions	You can interchange sessions
Total sessions	6	12	18

Our professional fees are due on the day of service. We appreciate the opportunity to serve your organization's needs. If you have any questions about this program, please feel free to contact me directly at (888) 987-5093. I look forward to working with you soon.

Sincerely,

Dr. Jesse W. Jackson III
Top-Rated School Staff Trainer and Clinical Therapist

The Parent Leadership Institute

EMPOWERING PARENTS TO MET THE CHALLENGES OF THE 21ST CENTURY
The Fathers, Single Mother & Grandparent Institute Seminar Series
consist of (10) seminars which will address the following specialty
areas:

Session #1   How To Raise A Son Who Is Without His Father: How Single
               Mothers & Grandparents Can Communicate With, Motivate
               And Keep Our Male Students Focused On Education.

Session #2   How to Discipline Your Son And Get The Results You Want.

Session #3   Parents & Teachers Working Together: How Parents Can
               Effectively Support School Staff.

Session #4   How To Improve Male Academic Performance. The
               Characteristics Of A High Risk Youth For Academic Failure
               And How To Keep Males Interested & Involved In Their
               Education.

Session #5   Father's Day, Bringing Men Back To The School: Why Fathers
               Are Important In The Life Every Human Being.

Session #6   The System: Why Boys End Up In Jail & How To Keep Your
               Son Out Of Jail and Get Him Into College.

Session #7   How To Find, Be Found, And Build A Strong Marriage
               Relationship & Stay Together Forever.

Session #8   "Are My Kids Having Sex?" What Parents Must Teach Their
               Children About Sex.

Session #9   Are My Kids Smoking WEED?" Why So Many Youth Are
               Smoking Marijuana & What We Can Do About It.

Session #10   Challenge TO Succeed: How To Help Your Children Find The
               RIGHT Path of College & Career Success.

Time: Each seminar 60 to 120 minutes in length.

All Schools Must Schedule A Minimum of Two Sessions

Call for individual or total program cost. **We will accommodate any
financial arrangement that needs to be made for your school.** For
more information concerning scheduling a seminar, seminar fees and
packages, please feel free to contact me directly at 888-987-5093 or 248
842-5041. I look forward to working with you soon.

Dr. Jesse W. Jackson III
Success Consultant & Clinical Therapist